THE DROWNED BOOK

Sean O'Brien grew up in Hull. He is Professor of Creative
Writing at Newcastle University. He has published five
collections of poetry, most recently *Downriver* (Picador, 2001),
which won the Forward Prize for best collection. *Cousin Coat:
Selected Poems, 1976–2001* appeared in 2002. His book of essays,
The Deregulated Muse (Bloodaxe), was published in 1998, as was
his acclaimed anthology *The Firebox: Poetry In Britain And Ireland
After 1945* (Picador). His most recent work is a verse translation
of Dante's *Inferno* (Picador, 2006). His verse plays include
a version of Aristophanes' *The Birds* (2002) and *Keepers of
the Flame* (2003).

THE DROWNED BOOK

Sean O'Brien

PICADOR

First published 2007 by Picador
an imprint of Pan Macmillan Ltd
Pan Macmillan, 20 New Wharf Road, London N1 9RR
Basingstoke and Oxford
Associated companies throughout the world
www.panmacmillan.com

ISBN 978-0-330-44762-1

9 8 7 6 5 4 3 2

A CIP catalogue record for this book is available from
the British Library.

Typeset in 11 /14.5pt Dante MT
Designed by Macmillan Design Department

Printed and bound in Great Britain by
Mackays of Chatham plc, Chatham, Kent

In Memory of Irene O'Brien 1920–2007

Acknowledgements

Answering Back, British Council New Writing, Metre, Miracle and Clockwork, Magnetic North, Moving Worlds, Near East Review, New Statesman, New Writing North, North by North East, Other Poetry, Poetry International, Poetry Ireland Review, BBC Poetry Proms, Poetry Review, The Rialto, Poetry London, Rivers, Times Literary Supplement.

'The Hand' was commissioned by the Calouste Gulbenkian Foundation for the anthology *Signs and Humours*, edited by Lavinia Greenlaw.

Contents

It took you forty years to reach this empty room.
Repaint the walls in arctic white.
Construct the desk. Draw up the spartan chair.
Then please repeat the question if you must.

The Apprehension

'Oh reason not the need'
— King Lear

'a protester was arrested under the act for "staring at a building".'
— George Monbiot, the *Guardian*, October 4th 2005

I apologize: I have by heart the names of clouds
For no good reason, and the waterways of Europe
Run three wet dimensions through my sleep,
And I confess my gaze has drifted on
To light on your discreet glass eye –
'The smallest Gothic window in the world' –
Above this still canal where Fascists walk
Their little dogs before they go to pray
For the deliverance of Flanders from the French.

Supreme Commissioner, your world of crime
Extends from Vistula to Finisterre
And in your tower at Bruges-la-Morte
You're early at your desk to know it all.
The relict of theology and lists,
How like a god you occupy the pause
Between intent and act, the subject and its sign,
How comprehensive the disdain to which
Compassion has migrated now.

But my concerns are accidental, Commissaire:
The double wooden gate where CINEMA
Is painted in that lettering first found
Between the wars: the bowed brick wall above,
About to yawn and split and fetch
The whole place down in one slow blink –
But not this evening. Now the lamps
Beside the Théâtre Grand sustain Magritte's
Miraculous and sourceless dusk-aubade,

Now blonde girls zip with flying skirts
Across the cobblestones on iron bicycles:
Rooms wait for them, and voices on the stairs, and sleep,
Where I imagine rain is merely falling too.
See: they let slip their pillow-books, whose names
I must invent, as if it mattered, sir,
The way it does to you, whose only energy
Is fear, that will forbid the world
Its momentary love and happenstance.

Water-Gardens

Water looked up through the lawn
Like a half-buried mirror
Left out by the people before.

There were faces in there
We had seen in the hallways
Of octogenarian specialists,

Mortality-vendors consulted
On bronchial matters
In rot-smelling Boulevard mansions.

We stood on their lino
And breathed, and below us
The dark, peopled water

Was leaning and listening.
There on the steps of the cellar,
Black-clad Victorians

Were feeding the river with souls.
They left us their things,
Reefs of blue ware

In the elder-clumps,
Tins full of rust in the shed,
And on the bookshelves

English poets, all gone damp
With good intentions, never read.
Their miles of flooded graves

Were traffic jams of stone
Where patient amphibian angels
Rode them under, slowly.

The voices came back
From sinks and gratings,
The treasure seekers

Gone downstairs, while all the time
In King Death's rainy garden
We were playing out.

River-doors

River-doors are not sea-doors. They open
Through mirrors and library shelves,
Through glasshouse sweat and damp attic walls.

They are the isomers of boredom.
Fleeing through a river-door the adult world's critique
You will hear the foul yawn of low tide caught

Au naturel in its khaki-tripe skin
Between the dented ironclad revetments
Of Drypool and Scott Street:

Barges, drowned dogs, drowned tramps, all are
Subdued to its element, worked
Into the khaki, with ropes and old staithes,

Estuarine polyps and leathery excrescences
No one has thought of a name for.
So much for childhood. Later you sit

From the long afternoon to the full moon's evening,
Blowing your dole on the landlord's voice:
At high tide, he says, in that intimate gurgling tone,

The river revisits his cellar,
Caressing the chains of the exciseman's ghost
Where he swings between this world and water's; but no,

It is never convenient to go down and see for yourself
How the river might stand at the foot of the steps.
The problem's the safety. The wife. It's the council,

He says, giving off the warm odour of bullshit.
However, you seem to be drinking the river in mild
And be eating its fruits from the pickled-egg jar

And as the product of refreshment hear
The river-door quietly open downstairs
Under the weight of the waters.

Eating the Salmon of Knowledge from Tins

The open drains began a long way off
As chalky freshets coming off the Wolds

– But by the time the city had its way
The water, if you glimpsed it, looked as thick
As jelly from a tin of Sunday ham.
A brick would shake it slowly
While the shawl of sputum-algae
Gathered up its threads again
And went on rotting from within.

– But it was water so we fished.
The drains are buried now – bulldozered down
To thin black seams that when it's wet
Climb up to drown the ground again

– But in the drought of 1959
They were polio rivers, street-long
Inch-deep stinks with one black fish,
The Witch Doctor we chased for weeks
From street to street with nets and jars.
At six p.m., TV, the facts in black and white,
Sick districts where the numbers
Epidemically rose – not ours

– But not far, a dozen streets downstream.
I think we took it in. We washed our hands
Then hurried back into the evening
To lean from the bridges
And study the lawns of green cress
With the salty heat still coming
Back off the water to madden the gnats.
Those treacly sewers bred no Grendels,
No fishers of children, no Bradys-in-waiting.

– But what was it made us a little afraid
In those huge summer dusks
Where the sun and the moon
Stood on opposite sides of the heavens
And clocks stopped at curfew?
They must have been down in the shade
On that wrong-angled sycamored bend
Where at the road the water slid
For thirty feet between the culvert's jaws,
And came out in a different light.

– But in those days the murderers
Came from elsewhere. We could read
Their bad names in the bits of *The People*
That rustled in dusty hedge-bottoms.
Diana Dors was guilty by association.
Crime, sex, the smell that wasn't fish.
Then we went back to fishing, staring down
Into the viscid stink as it got dark.

By Ferry

The ferry, *The Waverley*, churns on the sandbar.
In New Holland harbour the jellyfish
Hang in the murk at the jetty
Like plastic rain-hoods –
A race of drowned aunties
Come back to chastise us
For something we don't know we've done yet.

Sea Area Humber: poor visibility.
The jaws of the estuary? Infernal the gloom.
And Lincolnshire beneath the rain?
A plate of cabbage
Laid down at the door of sulking Cleethorpes.
For the sea had gone away
Round that great corner of the map,
Leaving us wormcasts and Biblical distance
With skeleton crews
Dancing hornpipes on islands of birdshit.

Drains

In drains begin responsibilities.
– Joseph Chamberlain

Sites of municipal vaticination,
Vents for the stench of the underworld.
In dreams we are digested there
And 'in that Catholic belly curled'.

There we are sunk for Barbaricchio's crew
To heft upon their tuning-forks.
We dream too much. We talk too much.
The future of the market lies in corks.

Re-edify me, drains. Give me again
The under-city's grand designs.
Let me explore your slimy malls,
Your long drops and your flooded mines.

Some say the drains are heaven's guts,
Out progress intestinal.
Wherever peristalsis leads
The outcome will be final.

A Coffin-Boat

In Memory of Barry MacSweeney

Today you must go for a walk in the dark. Go in
Where the stream by the graveyard falls
Into the tunnel and hurries off hoarse with graffiti.
You will be hauling a brass-handled narrowboat,
Mounted with twin candelabra, containing
A poet who managed to drink himself dead,
With heroic commitment, at fifty-one.
Packed up with books and manuscripts and scotch,
In his box from the Co-op, a birthright of sorts.

Get used to the visible stink. It will cling
In a tissue of soot to your hair. Get used
To the silence that stares and says nothing,
A graveyard of clocks with the time on the tips
Of their verdigris'd tongues. You should neither
Look back nor examine your luminous gaze
In the water. This place (the word is used loosely)
Gives off an air of religion decayed
To aesthetics and worse. At least one of everything
Finds its way here to this copyright Hell.
Item jar of cloudy eyes; item, carved
From bone, a grove of hatstands; item,
Detachment of ambient gargoyles with knouts;
Miscellaneous slick coils of excrement
And rag. And down the dripping galleries
Cartoons of howling inmates hang for sale

Between the stacks of disused literature,
Including some of his – and curiosity
May set him knocking on the lid for one more read,
But don't you stop: down here's the speechless
History of everything and nothing,
Poetry's contagious opposite. Go on
To the imaginary light.

                    Much later, far up,
Cries of gulls; a weedy birdlimed gate
That opens on the Ouseburn's curdled trench. Go on.
A mile upstream the tide turns back
Round weedy knobs of brick and stone
And clags of grot that wind themselves on mooring-rings.
Here is the rubbled anonymous slipway, left
Among black warehouses designed to look
Resigned and stoic in the hands of lawyers.
They are waiting out the era of unwork
When all the clocks run sideways
And the workers are walking the roads daylong
(From famine road to Scotswood's but a step)
Or imbibing the milk of amnesia. This place
Will be nothing, was nothing, is never, its tenses
Sold off one by one until at last the present stands
Alone like a hole in the air. But still
This is history, this silence and disuse,
This non-afternoon, and it must also serve
Biography – to whit, your man's, for here he goes
Out through the space left for comments made
Over the coffin. You and I, my friend,

And all the rest have who found their way here
Down Jesmond Dene and under Byker Bridge –
We must give an account of our presence.
We shall have to find words for the matter. So, then:
We've come on account of inadequate answers
To phone calls at midnight, to phone calls
Ignored and left ringing. We've witnessed
Italianate umbrage in bar-rooms, read
The poems of recovery and relapse and wondered
What in God's name could be done, and as we did so
Heard the rumour and the death confirmed.
We remember his anger and hurt – and our pity,
That futile and dutiful feeling that hasn't a map
But relies on itself to continue, that shrivelled
When met with the fact of his rage like a bucket of lava
Flung over the listener. Rage. It was tireless
And homeless, and though it walked out on the body
It could not be quenched by affection
Or drink: even now, at the death and beyond, oh yes
It must carry on dragging its grievances into the dark,
For the want of a nail, of a home, of a matchbox,
A drum of pink paraffin, anything fiery enough
To let the man rest by the waters of Tyne.

The River in Prose

i

Down to that area of retired water, among gridlocked stone docks barely the size of football pitches, fed by the tides through broken lock-gates which the mud is digesting. The word 'inshore' – jaunty river-coppers hooking what turns out to be only a sack from the wake of the ferry. Jaunty Humber pilots squawking over the radio: bad weather in the mouth of the estuary, miles away.

Identify, please, the point, not officially recorded, at which a barge ceases to be simply unvisited and at rest and becomes derelict; becomes an interior the water goes over at leisure, something condemned by the fact it can never be water. Does somebody look at a kitchen clock in a nearby street and give in to indifference, lassitude, despair, economics? Is there *any* element of deliberation, or is the barge's history simply exhausted, something effaced with the illusion of speed produced by inattention?

ii

Say: *here is a dream of extinction.* Say: *it carried coals from Selby, bashing through the swell like a Merrimack boat, part perhaps of Zachariah Pearson's dream of blockade-running empire, of the manutenency of slavery undertaken, from the city whose MP was the abolitionist Wilberforce, whose house of exhibited shackles is a mere five hundred yards away. The reformer stood at the end of his garden, thirty years before the War Between the States, inwardly calling on the Creator for assistance and looking down into the Hull, while round the corner the barge or its ancestor was going out to work in the cause of money. Water lies between the plank floor of the cabin and the hull, sieving the stinking ballast twice daily. The tide comes in through the broken lock-gate, investing every rotten inch of a vessel so* 'much decayed' *as no longer to merit a name.* You come here in 1959, in perfect ignorance.

iii

The rivermen. Rivermen's pubs, where the river is penned in the cellars. Somebody bit off the head of the landlord's parrot.

Is this the Russian consulate? *No, this is the Club Lithuania, Dogger Street Branch. Are you a member?* No, but I've sailed through pancake ice on a Baltic ferry while Wagnerian bridge-pillars loomed past in the fog and been very afraid. Will that do? *You have to get signed in. You have to sit there on that sofa with that girl while she ignores you. Here at the Club Lithuania we specialize in continuous disappointment. We never close. Just sit there for the present. Eat your sild.*

Upstream, the riverbank and its hinterland are an annexe of Belgian Symbolism: low, grey-green, belated, formally a place but in fact an end to places, formally a flood-plain but in fact somewhere geography has finished dealing with. *No Fishing,* says a sign by the side of a dyke. Cannibals in skiffs come rowing smoothly down at dusk, with a barely a drip in the grey waters of the right-angled network –

The Mere

Its poplars and willows and sludge. Its gnat-clouds.
Smell of cooling animal at dusk. Grey-greenness.
Soup-suspension. Its having been
Here all along. It is nowhere, serves nothing, lives
On your behalf when you are absent.
Now they want to drain it. Now anticipate
The day when you will have to set this place
Apart, with sticks and stones.
Not for the mere the glum fate of
A run-of-the-mill Sussex valley.

Nor any great claims. No leverage sought
Beneath the aesthetics of crims from the deadlands
Whose task is to *make good* a landscape,
To drain it and extract the name
It never had. It's just
That you have to save something –
A fence-post, the shape of a firebreast
Nailed high on a wall by your ignorant gaze:
They will add up to love in a hand of decades.
Grounds for affray, are they not? So too the mere.

– Life is a word you can sometimes remember
And might never use, but that's
Nobody's business. Cracked heads and burnt hands,
On behalf of the mere. Soup by the brazier.
Standing pool, body of water, formerly
Arm of the sea, now chiefly *poet.* and *dial.*,
Anonymous, here with us now
In the order of things – this is what
You will find you have chosen,
If choice is the word, to defend.

The River Road

Come for a walk down the river road,
For though you're all a long time dead
The waters part to let us pass

The way we'd go on summer nights
In the times we were children
And thought we were lovers.

The river road led to the end of it all –
Stones and pale water, the lightship's bell
And distance we never looked into.

A long time gone
And the river road with it.
No margin to keep us in mind.

For afterlife, only beginning, beginning,
Wide, dark waters that grow in the telling,
Where the river road carries us now.

Three Lighthouses

for Ellen Phethean

When their history's over,
The rivermouth offers these lighthouses
Sheltered employment: watch, reflect

And let the square white towers
Take the light laid on at dusk and dawn
By Scottish colourists –

White that is blue,
That is nothing at all,
That is water and air,

And that says, although never
In so many words,
That the world we have lived in

Is real, and therefore does not lie
Beyond the dream of touching,
But places its light in our hands.

This evening the ferry will carry us
Home with the workers off shift,
An old couple, a mother and child,

And whatever our dead friends
Would say if they stood
In the bow alongside us, remember,

To take in the sight, coming back
On the gathering waters that slide
To the mouth of the Tyne, where the world

Is beginning and ending:
Three lighthouses wearing the weather,
In each of them a table laid

With rosemary and rue,
So that the dead may sit at peace
And watch with us tonight.

Grey Bayou

When I return to Grey Bayou, the mud-kingdom
Fed by dykes and chalky run-off
I would like my fire-ship to nose ashore

Beside the sheds near Little Switzerland
In memory of lust among the quarry-pits
A thousand years ago, before the bridge.

It is roads now, clover-leafs, pillars,
And only the bayou remains of that world,
Its reed-beds caged against the shifting channels,

Though the eternal flame to industry still burns,
Tiny like a funerary torch, far off
Downriver on the southern side, among the palms.

I would like a flotilla of tar-coloured barges
To happen past then, inbound for Goole,
The odd crewman furtively smoking and staring,

As though an ancient prophecy is vindicated now
When the fools who denied it are dead or in jail.
For this is the place, the rivermen know,

In which nothing need happen especially.
A boat burning out on the flats
Belongs with one more fording on horseback,

The first cries of love in the elder-grove,
Dark mild and cigarettes, the Mississippian
Expanses of the unknown Grey Bayou,

Its grey-brown tides, its skies
That dwarf the bridge and with their vast
Indifference honour and invoke the gods.

Song: Habeas Corpus

PAGES: *What are ye, scabs?*
WATCH: *The watch.*

Oh lock me in the deepest jail
And throw away the key.
The nation's desperate to be saved
From 'elements' like me.
There's none so blind,
We think you'll find
As those who cannot see.

So you be judge and jury,
Let the trial I won't attend
Take up your valuable time
And damn me in the end.

Forget about due process,
The evidence, the court:
The evil I've committed
Is as secretive as thought.

Just think, if I'm not found in time,
Then I might perpetrate
An absolutely novel crime
Known only to the state –

An act more terrible because
It hasn't happened yet –

For in our time the future tense
Will be the major threat.

Dear Sergeant, save me from myself
Before I reach the brink:
God knows what I might dream of,
Left alone to sit and think.

Cut deep into the cortex
And declare: *His brain is sick.*
He's going to have to take the cure
Supplied at Belmarsh nick.

Of course he *doesn't know he's ill:*
It's not his business, right?
Now warders, take this villain down
Until he sees the light.

Condemn me in absentia
And fix my tariff high,
Then tell my friends I've gone away
But gave no reason why.

Oh I shall dine on week-old bread
And drink from a cardboard cup.
If anyone should hear this song,
Just say I made it up:

Justice? Justice may be blind
But Ministers are blinder,
Walking England's frightened streets
With a leather-coated minder.

Now join me, honest citizens,
Let's drink to unknown crime –
We'll all be on the inside soon,
One nation doing time.
Burn out our brains,
Lock us in chains
To prove to us we're free –
There's none so blind,
We think you'll find,
As one who cannot see.

The Lost War

The saved were all ingratitude,
The lost would not lie down:
Reborn, their sacred rage renewed,
They razed the fallen town

And in the graveyard made their stand
Just east of heaven's gate.
We are the same. It is all one
Whom we exterminate.

Timor Mortis

Into the pit go all Estates,
All princes, pimps and potentates,
The fiend next door, the BBC –
The living and those yet to be,
Eminem, Ms Ruby Wax
And Robert Johnson's vanished tracks,
Donald Rumsfeld, Richard Perle,
Madonna and the Duke of Earl,
Occam's razor, Charlie Chan,
Lord Lucan and the bogey man,
Mister Tony, Conrad Black,
The orchestra from *Crackerjack*,
The Andrews Sisters, Clausewitz,
That wasname who gets on your tits,
Captain Nemo, Guildenstern
And suchlike planks booked in to burn,
De Tocqueville and Thomas Hobbes,
Ascetics, charvers, Rent-a-Gobs,
Boadicea, Brian Clough –
The world itself is not enough
To satisfy the hungry void,
Though 'housewives and the unemployed'
Slip down with Marx and Jackie O.
Last sitting, everything must go –
Indifference and appetite,
The dimwit armies of the night,

Dispensers of banal advice,
Kate Moss and Condoleezza Rice,
Machine Gun Kelly, Iron Mike,
The Beemer and the butcher's bike,
Wallace Stevens, you and me,
The Devil and the deep blue sea,
The wonks who work the cutting edge,
Immanuel Kant and Percy Sledge,
With Peter Pan, the Golden Horde,
All travellers not yet on board
Plus those who think it don't apply,
Who witter, witter, 'I'm, like, *why?*'
Join Zeno, Zog and Baudelaire
As conscripts of *le grand nowhere* –
Some on ice and some on fire,
Some with slow piano wire,
Screaming, weeping, brave as fuck
And absolutely out of luck.
My friends, Lord Death is cruel but fair:
He loves it when there's nothing there,
No Baghdad and no Superbowl,
No *langue* and likewise no *parole*,
No Gulf Stream and no polar ice,
No evidence of Paradise.
His only mood's imperative.
He knows our names and where we live.
He sees no reason to record
The names of those whose bones are stored
In his extensive cellarage:

They are unwritten, like this page.
Come now, and board his empty ark –
What need of poems in the dark?

Sheol

It was different then, oh you cannot imagine
For one thing the war when these three generations
Were crushed into bone-dust one teatime.
These were lost at sea and this one trapped
On the floor of a lock till his eyes burst out.
To say nothing of murder, by shovel and arsenic,
By random malevolence snatching them up
At the roadside to boil them away, beyond
Sex, beyond names and belief. Or this child
From a cupboard, whom nobody killed, not exactly.

A Little Place They Know

To say that the sessions are long is to call
The Crusades 'an affray'. To say that you don't
Understand what the hell's going on
Is like finding Babel 'a little confusing'.
Here in the old world the clocks can run
Backwards or sideways at random, and when,
On the brink of despair, your turn is called –
By then you hardly recognize your name.

How suddenly empty the chamber becomes,
How discreet the Mercedes that spirit
Their regretful delegations homeward.
Now the clocks look at you pointedly. Quick!
You read to seven dead Bulgarians
And then they read to you, and afterwards
They take you to a little place they know
In a hole in the wall of the graveyard.

You wake now. The plates have been cleared. Your hosts,
Obedient to curfew, have departed.
The moon waits, and down at the end of the street
In its washed-out blue engineer's jacket
The sea too is tidelessly waiting, so
All you can hear where the waves ought to break
Is the fizz of butt-ends in the water
Drowning faint renditions of 'Volare'.

Yes, you tell yourself, let's go – *Thalassa,*
Thalassa, you know my true name – the stars
Awake when you and I take ship. But this
Is the shore that comes back through the mist
And the name of your death for this evening
Is Constantin Harbour, 1916,
Museum and slaughterhouse, beautiful hole
In the wall of the graveyard. Do step aboard.

Symposium at Port Louis

Drifting ashore on a salt-cracked book-box,
Buoyed up with Byron and Shakespeare,
Once again we ship Coles' Notes
To Newcastle. No home these days
For obsolete litterateurs,
Only temporary anchorage
Deep in the southern hemisphere.
Safe for now in the cyclone's eye,
With scribbled notes on a borrowed page
And winging it like Hannay,
It seems our task is to discover whether
Concordia et Progressio can
Ever be more than contraries
Yoked by violence together.
– Someone would know, as your man
Remarked. We have come a long way
To sit in this elegant council chamber
Emblazoned with creole
Chevaux-de-mer; to hear
A grave centenarian entrepreneur
Set down his ledger and appeal
To his gods, to whit: Carlyle
And Chesterton and Masefield's 'Cargoes'.
Here the rolling English drunkard
Looks in secret at his watch and longs
For a sober world of prose,
Where objects are allowed

To be themselves, and stern embargoes
Seal the ports of commerce and of dreams
To grand abstraction and the soul alike:
Let Jesuit and Mameluke
Politely anchor in the roads
Till Mrs Hawoldar decides
To fire the sunset gun and bring
Proceedings to a close.
    The names of former mayors
Are allegorical in spades:
Monsieur Charon, Messrs Forget,
Tranquille and Martial. Their shades
Are words alone and yet persist
To haunt the carnival,
To make this page a sheet of foam
Dissolving as it slides
Across the reef, till danger meets
The sea-change into pleasure, when the mind
For all its radical intent gives in
To ocean light and Phoenix beer,
Reef-walking fishermen at dawn
Who glide and strut like Sega's
Dancing girls in skirts of flouncing surf –
And in the steady winter sunshine
Distances so wholly theoretical
That fear and ecstasy are one.
Yet on the *menu touristique*
There are items never mentioned:
Race and class and money
And the iron status quo,

Concerning which guests do not speak:
Out of this place, tradition states,
Desire not to go. Meanwhile
Like peasants in Van Gogh,
Cane-cutters with their cutlasses
Relax at noon beside the road
And over dinner at Grand Baie
Among the careless trove of pearls
And smirks and scallop-sconces
The Chinese minister confers
His poems on three hundred Hindu guests,
As Muslim families in fear secrete
Kalashnikovs between the joists
And Creole says what people mean,
Not what they ought, and all day long
The smell comes up the cracks
In concrete-covered gutters –
Rum and Phoenix, poverty
And wasted time, because
The afterlives of colonies
Are everywhere the same.
Inland at Cascade Chamarel
The rainbow will explode
And Ganesh, god of memory,
Will accommodate it all,
Gazing calmly inwards
Underneath the waterfall.

   This stormy chamber in its garden is
A southern cell where Prospero
Might set to right the grievances

Of this extended family –
But this time let the magus drown his book
Before he bids us all adieu.
Let poison run back up the leaf,
The will resume its innocence, and all
Before they go join hands downstage
To take the sea's applause and look
Once more at how the waves come in
As ever, faithful to the shore
And yet asleep
As soundly as the drowned men in the deeps
Beyond the coral shelf,
To whom the upper world
Is sealed, as firmly
As the mind of God himself.

The Them

They like to do the leaving. You're what's left.
Forever on the phone for Lebensraum,
They're outraged: is this world so understaffed
It cannot meet the needs of the elect
For engineered consent and odalisques
To match these selfless gifts of steaming Zaum?
And these insane requests to be ignored:
What did you seriously expect?
Look now: the tanks are massing on your desk;
The gods must be garrotted or adored.

Proposal For a Monument to the Third International

In Memory of Keith Morris

'All that is solid melts into air'

SOLO
I was dreaming in a station of the Metro.
The railbeds were freezing rivers of blood
With bergs of fat, where millions knelt
To eat and drink,

CHORUS
              and it was good.

SOLO
What are they singing,

CHORUS
                the crowd

SOLO
That is never the same from moment to moment,

CHORUS
The crowd

SOLO
        whose faces vanish
And re-form, who have no names,

CHORUS
The crowd with its mouthful of blood,
The crowd

SOLO
          In which the million you and I are lost
Like information buried in an archive?
What is that song?

CHORUS
We are buried alive.
We are not what was meant.
Let history finish.
Let stones become stars. Let the stars speak.

SOLO
Let those inside the walls of adamantine
Ice-cream reply in a deafening whisper
As ice writes its name in the river again.
History, history, what are our names?

Little sister, tell me, can you see
Hosts of steam-angels, racing away
Down the blue Moskva at wavetop height
To confer their industrial blessings
On fur and glass, on felt and skin
And the old man who wearily enters
The forest of coats at the end of the day
To come back with ours? Likewise the babushka
Sweeping dead steam from the underpass

Is blessed and when the state withers will stand
With her brothers and sisters
On the wintry glacis by the Kremlin wall
By the site of executions.

CHORUS
The city runs like science fiction backwards.
Putin in his sheet-steel chariot
Is brandishing a grail of blood and vlaast
On a stem of twisted dragon-tails.

SOLO
I rode to the twenty-ninth floor
Of the Hotel Ukraina, then climbed the last steps
To the last locked room
Where a camera obscura portrayed the night city
As Stalin might dream it himself
From one of the seven dark stars he cast
So high that the heavens themselves
Were extinguished.

I turned to descend and there by the door
Was a wizened old man, sitting smoking.
A red fire-bucket was full of his ash.
He wore two watches and between his eyes
A bullet hole.
He looked indifferently through me.
Brothers, this is all I can recall.

CHORUS
The Tambov wolf shall be your comrade now.
This is your station now.
Press to the doors.

SOLO
Let us walk over the bridge
By the pool where the steam-angels
Spend their retirement.
Let us walk over the snow
In the field of dead statues.

We shall hand in our coats
To the dear old dead couple
Who add our black coats to the forest of coats
In the province of coats
And the bear Mikhail Semyonov
Presides in the court of the coats this day.

Shall we go in
And look at the art?

CHORUS
Up here is the modest proposal
A tower
A furnace
A children's amusement
Babel
And the key to all economies
When Eiffel took a potion he made this

SOLO
What is it made of?

CHORUS
Of matchwood and wire
Brown paper and misunderstanding.
This is no longer historical.
Art
And no longer historical,
Art
And can never remember the time.

SOLO
What shall we hope for?

CHORUS
To come here and see.
To have your curious half hour.
To go back through the crowd,

SOLO
To take our coats from the forest of coats
And tip the babushka
And walk to the Metro
And stand in the crowd between trains
When the blood is not running.

CHORUS
To know
We are buried alive,
To know
We are not what was meant.
Let history finish.
Let stones become stars
And let the stars speak.

Valedictory

Those living and those yet to be
Are all her immortality:
The subjects of the world she made
Still speak her language, still afraid
      To change it.
She saw her people as they were:
Don't-Cares who can't be made to care:
These sentimental hypocrites
Let her, their true-blue Clausewitz
      Arrange it.

Let poverty without parole
Replace the right to draw the dole.
Let coppers pulling triple time
Turn opposition into crime
      At Orgreave.
Let the *General Belgrano*,
Sunk to save our sheep, our guano,
Mark the freezing south Atlantic
As the empire's last romantic
      War grave.

Let children learn no history
These days, but only how to be
As economically astute
As all the dealers snorting toot
      For dinner,

Desperate to anticipate
Like destiny the nation state's
Ineluctable decline
To client status: *I me mine*,
             The winner.

Branch libraries and playing fields
Deliver rather slower yields
Than asset-stripping mountebanks
Can rake in flogging dope and tanks:
             Great Britain!
Strange: no one nowadays admits
To voting in the gang of shits
Who staffed her army of the night:
Our history, it seems, is quite
             Rewritten.

When it comes to telling lies
The change is hard to recognize.
What can't be hidden can be burned.
She must be gratified: we've learned
             Her lesson.
Now when some sanctimonious ape
Says, *No, there never was a tape,
A bribe, a private meeting with*
Et cetera, where are you, Smith
             And Wesson?

Let the histories receive
This lady, who did not believe
In treating with the TUC,
In guff about 'society',
        In turning.
Bid farewell to one who knew
Precisely what the world should do
In every case, without remorse,
And let her lie, unless of course
        She's burning:

– For though we are prohibited
From speaking evil of the dead
Might her conspicuous contempt
For weakness render her exempt
        From pity?
Tempted though we are, we must
Be merciful as well as just.
Let ignorance be iron-willed:
The task is always to rebuild
        Our city.

Fantasia on a Theme of James Wright

There are miners still
In the underground rivers
Of West Moor and Palmersville.

There are guttering cap-lamps bound up in the roots
Where the coal is beginning again.
They are sinking slowly further

In between the shiftless seams,
To black pools in the bed of the world.
In their long home the miners are labouring still –

Gargling dust, going down in good order,
Their black-braided banners aloft,
Into flooding and firedamp, there to inherit

Once more the tiny corridors of the immense estate
They line with prints of Hedley's *Coming Home*.
We hardly hear of them.

There are the faint reports of spent economies,
Explosions in the ocean floor,
The thud of iron doors sealed once for all

On prayers and lamentation,
On pragmatism and the long noyade
Of a class which dreamed itself

Immortalized by want if nothing else.
The singing of the dead inside the earth
Is like the friction of great stones, or like the rush

Of water into newly opened darkness. My brothers,
The living will never persuade them
That matters are otherwise, history done.

The Thing

The ring of fire in Act Three should actually
Evoke the SS chapel at Schloss Wewelsberg,
i.e. not Johnny Cash. The 'problem with Mephisto'

Is not in fact a problem with Mephisto, but with you,
'My friend', and while I'm not at all inflexible
Or precious where the script's concerned, the 'difference

It will make' if Mephisto is played as though
From Hartlepool is that you will be dead.
Apart from that I think we're up to speed.

Thom Gunn

We set out to explore the poison root,
To etch the brain with new cartography,
The harbour-glitter and the wine-dark sea.
The only rule was endless latitude.
Let the unready falter and retire –
We loved and feared your eager solitude,
The city as a man-made absolute,
A sunset grid of immanent desire.

Let those of us who longed to board but failed
Salute you *in absentia*, Captain Gunn,
Now attitude and argosy have sailed
Beyond the west. You had no other course
But mustering your whole 'hot, wasteful' force
To beach in the annihilating sun.

Serious Chairs

Upright, blue-cushioned, with curved wooden arms,
Waiting like habitués of vivas and auditions,
The serious chairs are never all taken –
Always there is someone missing, caught
In a delayed appointment, lost to us
In the stony glare of long summer streets,
Behind whose darkened windows other rooms like this
With their unbreathing patience hold
Their half-audiences, too, beneath the grave
Half-decent portraits of the wise and their mustachios
Reposing in the chairs of other days. Shall we begin?
All knowledge is a tragedy. Already we digress.

Far better to be nobody at all than serve
The secret cult of one's own personality,
As no one would deny, yet even here
In the serious chairs – or is it here especially? –
The friction of the self against these others
And the facts can seem intolerable, almost,
Because some radical injustice means
You may at last be absolutely wrong.
So the girl in the high-collared blouse sits
Knitting and worrying, and the man behind her
Struggles with the lifelong rage that makes
His Ernest Bevin spectacles expand alarmingly,

And lurking one row back in restless immobility
The ancient independent scholar knows
What no one else has grasped – that angels
Are not so terrible in fact, or not to him,
Who has taken the trouble to make their acquaintance.
Yet in this setting he is too considerate
To tell us that if he so chose he could
Address us now, complacently, in tongues of flame –
For he means to outlive us, to sit here alone
On that blue cushion, that serious chair,
With knowledge like a skull inside a box,
And wait for no one, patiently, like this.

Three Facetious Poems

Sung Dynasty

My lover tells me that when autumn comes
He will fashion me a boat of cherry blossom:
There's no way I'm getting in that.

Why The Lady

She represents the rose and universal hope;
The fiery core; herself before the court
Of man's conceit – exonerated, free;
The hidden bud for which the dead will rise;
The ruby on the salt bed of the sea;
A kiss. That's why the lady is a trope.

Of Rural Life

Pigs. Chickens. Incest. Murder. Boredom. Pigs.

Lost Song of the Apparatus

The curved platform of Cullen Station, 1963.
The house on the right, beyond the station building,
Was a typical L-plan stationmaster's home.

67 *'With elaborate art Virgil gives his language*
Here the appearance of careless ease.'
Portessie / Buckie / Aultmore*

*known as Forgie

Ladysbridge Asylum – Near Banff.
Many will remember the call
'Change for Fochabers Town.'

At the platform to the left of the station building.
70. *namque…*] *'for the well-known martial note of*
Harsh-sounding brass urges on the laggards.'

Hopeman 14 September 1931
72 *fractos…*] Cf. the well-known line of Ennius,
At tuba terribili sonitu tarantara dixit.

Burghead (first) 10th October 1892
Greens of Drainie November 1859
Coleburn* – *known as Coleburn Platform

Until April 1967/ 'A badly sited station
Some distance from the village.'
Kildrummie Platform/ Taucher's Platform/

Towiemore Station, August 1966.
It was still open at the time –
The carriage body served as a waiting room!

Drummuir Curling Pond Platform –
Date unknown. There was
130 *rarum in dumis*] *'here and there amid the bushes'*

A branch line to the harbour
On the east side of this building but
It ceased to be used in the 1880s.

410. 'and melting into insubstantial
water will be gone.' **393**. *trahantur*]
expresses the sequence or connection

Of events, and suggests the thread of destiny.
394. *quippe...*] *'for surely such is the will of Neptune'*.
Both 'quippe' and 'visum est' are stately.

Five Railway Poems for Birtley Aris

1. Inheritance

In this compartment you discover
The poems of De La Mare,
Left open at 'The Railway Junction',

The late-nineteenth-century rhetoric
Turning from art into history now
As you snuff up the gutter:

From here through tunnelled gloom
the track divides. These days
The grim-faced keeper with his gun

Patrols the madhouse walls,
The drooling curate's shut within,
And the bow-legged bridegroom,

Seduced and abandoned –
He must be you, confined for good
To this thin medium,

To coal-smoke, oil-sweat, gusty corridors
That thunder onto viaducts
Flung across gulfs of industrial fog,

Then into howling tunnel-mouths
As if each darkness were the last of all.
What use are your gifts now,

Your cage-bird and kind word,
Your old-world fidelity,
Infinite patience?

2. Cherchez la Femme

Trains cry in the night across fields
And bombed sidings – nearer, further,
Promises blowing their smoke in your eyes.
By now you would give anything.
And still she does not come.
' . . . *all things that thou wouldst praise*
Beauty took from those who loved them
In other days.'

Beauty's a practical girl.
She can bathe in a bare two inches
Then, dodging the bombers, slip out
To the ball in a gown made of blackout.
Cherchez la femme.
She leaves the Bible in its drawer,
A pair of stockings on the shower-rail,
But nothing with her signature.

Now seek her in the stations of the capital,
Where all the girls impersonate that look,
Peremptory, amused, with always
Somewhere else to be.
Her handmaids serve a brutal faith.
Look in their eyes, night after night
Beneath the clock, and see: it is not
She who is invisible.

3. Yellow Happiness

The painting over the luggage rack –
Its yellow happiness, that blinded bay
Whose figures are dissolving in the waves.

Clearly life's not possible.
Let there be art, of a kind. Let Rimbaud
Go to ground in yellow Scarborough

In the bowels of the Grand Hotel
Among plongeurs and chambermaids.
He's there, he's in the frame –

As you are, *cherie*, you who stole
My happiness to wear that yellow dress
You threw aside to run into the sea.

One day the sea train will mean what it says,
Ploughing into the waves like a special effect
At the birth of a submarine Yorkshire,

And out of the wreck you will rise
On an open gold compact,
Quite naked except for the powder-puff

Stylishly saving your modesty.
Those not yet dead will acclaim you
Sea-Gipsy, calling your creatures below.

4. Bridge

It would be sacrilege to put a word
Into that open mouth, that waits
And does not wait, while nothing comes.

And how you envy it the right to be
A sketch of smoke and ash at dusk,
An England hoisted to the light again

To send its breath of bone and earth
Into the unborn world – this sunlit
Arch of dust, this faith without believers,

And its language no one speaks. It has
No time for us, for matters of the heart,
But looks down alleys lined with birch and sycamore

Towards uncomprehending distances,
Unblinkingly in both directions, always.

5. Reasonable Men

They are reasonable men,
The railway guard and the doctor's assistant,
Filling the compartment door
With reasonable arguments
For getting off next stop and going back
Until you feel the benefit.
The train is crawling diplomatically
Across the levels, vamping
On a chord of steam. A river
Swims up close like an encouragement.
The fishermen look up and look away.
Willow, poplar, aspen, locks, a pub
And there behind the early haze the whole
Implied immensity of England.
You will never find it now. You can recall
A scarecrow in a streaming silver field,
The doorman of Anglian distances
Not to be entered this side of paradise.
You sought the place on large-scale maps
But here you are. The train is entering
A wood of silver birch. It's intimate –
A hundred acres of discreet attentiveness.
If they were nurses now, these trees
Would fold their hands together and look down.

You've missed what the conductor said.
He looks at you across his kind moustache
As if you must see reason shortly.
Would that it were so. But having been
Important to the world by being young
You understand that your decline, if not
Explained, is somehow warranted: why else
Would you be sitting looking out
And catching in the window the concern
Of those to whom you might be anyone
Or nobody at all – a gadgee on the lam
From the electrodes? They may say
The Midnight Special does not run,
That no one is redeemed by going North.
You know they must be wrong: how else
Could this embarrassing unhappiness,
This history of oddments – not this station,
One quite like it – justify itself at all?

Railway Hotel

In Memory of Ken Smith

Why this hotel, and this town and this province of X
On this night in the Year of the Turnip? Why
This name and this face in the passport? Well?

Out there the foggy road still curves away
Across the railway tracks. Young birches in the sidings.
Sounds of shunting, off in the rusty damp.

The suitcase. Full of books? It could as easily
Be drill-bits, lenses, chocolate.
You must be travelling in something. *Time,*

You say, flicking the locks to inspect
The interior. Something that glows? You give
Nothing away. It goes under the bed again.

Down at the end of the hall is a wolf in a case,
Howling at the moon in 1910, illuminated
By the beer sign in the street. Perhaps

It went like this: you stopped for dinner here
To view the curiosities, and this
Was one of them. You never know.

At her high desk the red-haired proprietress
Sits in a draught with the radio doing a polka
To death, and once again she's gotten

Lipstick on her teeth. And nothing happens
For a hundred years but fog and shunting,
Lipstick and polkas, the half-lives

Of objects marooned by imagined
Utility. So, are we going, or what?

Grimshaw

November – Copper beeches bare – The gates
Shut fast against the poor – Disconsolate
Illumination shed by gasoliers –
Damp garden walls and hidden escritoires.

The northern master Grimshaw understood
Belatedness: the passing of an age
That does not pass. In mourning clothes, the road
Bends out of sight to meet its widowed world.

Indoors now, lamplit hands turn over cards
Or patiently inscribe a page that might
Beguile the moral thirst of half-mad girls
Before whom winter opens like a grave.

The night has barely started on the clock.
We see no one. No letters come but yours.
Write soon. Around the globe's great curve,
Ship me your opiates of ink, my love.

Rose

You sit there watching August burn away
The waxy, crumpled pages of the rose

You love too much but cannot keep, or wake
With any word you whisper in its ear:

And neither will its hundred burning tongues
Call out to you, not once, not ever, now.

Blue Night

Blue night. Enormous Arctic air. Orion's belt.
A geostationary satellite.
The birds all sheltering or flown.

The world is North, and turns its North Face
Pitilessly everywhere,
As deep as Neptune, local as the moon.

First came the fall and then the metaphor
No other island, then. No gift of grace.
For this alone is 'seriously there'.

Therefore. Therefore. Do not be weak.
They have no time for pity or belief,
The heavens, in their triumph of technique.

Transport

after Stefan George

This is the air of another planet.
Friends' faces, that greeted me lately,
Are gone in the dark.

The forest paths I loved
Are fading now –

        and you,
My beloved, bright ghost, even you
Who gave me all my pain, even you
Are eclipsed in this radiant night,

For the quarrels and uproar are over
And something beyond me
Commands me to awe:
        so the self
Burns, in the sound of no sound
And the ash offers praise
To abandon its voice
To a voice beyond hearing.

Dawn. Beyond the mountains rise
The sun and emptiness, the far
Blue gulf I am to cross if I believe,
A sea of burning ice –

Where I shall be one tongue of flame
Among the holy flame, a single note
Within the holy voice.

Abendmusik

This evening, Rilke at the harmonium
Plays sour chords of widowed expectation
Pedalled to infinity. Let it be now.
Everyone is here, discreetly,
Observing the stars through gaps in the curtains,
Down sightlines disrupted by bombazined women,
By shakos on piano-lids, by music-stands
And silver horns coffined in cases. Everyone.
An angel is promised; is promised.
The smell is the river in summer, the green earth
Laid bare to the heavens. An angel.
Heartless world, you alone persist.
You send us out into uttermost space
And exemplary silence. You promise an angel
To meet us, here in this room – let it be now –
In the stars, in the dusk-heavy pier-glass
Containing the river, those alders,
That perfect perfunctory curve of farewell
Whose only end is to contain our lives
Like Rilke's unresolving chords. Let it be now.
After so long an evening,
Star-blinded, deaf to the river,
Forgetting the names of our dead,
How can the Gräfin, the poet, the servant, the statesman,
That girl in the corner no longer attending,
Believe that the one we're awaiting,
Caught up in the curve of the river, the music,

The light of the stars from whose fires
We answer solitude with solitude, is here
Among us now and that its name is patience?

The Hand

A repeated procedure for Dupuytren's Contracture may
unavoidably result in stiffness and some loss of sensation.

My good right hand, farewell to you.
I must begin to take my leave,
And will depart through your extremity.
I cannot hold a friend's hand now,
Nor form a fist, nor open in a wave.
They say the only remedies
For what ails me are ailments too:
They had to kill the hand they fought to save.
Lie still and let me look at you.
You seem unmoved: I am the one undone,
And so let go of you, my hand.
Although you still extend on my behalf,
Now that my grasp of you is gone,
Nothing remains to comprehend.
Therefore I watch you endlessly
For your resemblance to the real,
And see the same smashed knuckle,
The scarring and the same club thumb,
The inability to feel
Made flesh, but unequipped for rage or love:
And yet you ache, as if with cold,
As armour might, remembering
Its heartlessness, its iron fist
Imprisoned in its iron glove.

After Rilke: To Holderlin

In Memory of Michael Donaghy

We may not stay, not even with the most familiar things.
No sooner is the image comprehended than the mind
Accelerates into the waiting emptiness: and therefore
Only in eternity shall we encounter lakes.
Falling is all we must hope for, falling
From the known into the guessed-at, falling further.

For you the hero, for you who forswore it, life
In its entirety was the insistent image;
And when you gave that life a name
The line would seal itself like destiny. Though even
In your gentlest word a death was resident,
The god who walked ahead would lead you out and over.

Wandering spirit, none wandered further.
The others are proud to keep house in small poems,
To linger in narrow comparisons. Professionals. You alone
Pull like the moon: see now, below it grows light, it grows dark,
Your landscape, the sacred and startled night-landscape
That you comprehend in your leaving. No one
Renounced this more nobly and no one
Restored it so nearly intact, or asked for less.
So too, in the years you stopped counting, you played
With an infinite joy, as though joy were not shut inside us,
But lay in the grass of this earth, without ownership, left by
                                        celestial children.

What the best desire you built without desire,
Brick on brick: and there it stood. And when it fell
It could not discompose you.
How can we, after this timeless example,
Mistrust life still, when we could learn
To sense from all that's passing now
The planet's inclination to the earth, the world to come?

Praise of a Rainy Country

In Memory of Julia Darling

The popular song that first season, remember,
Was *Rhythm of the Rain* by The Cascades.
In tower blocks on dripping summer evenings
The impossible girlfriends stood at their sinks
In slips and curlers, rinsing out their blouses
While it pleaded – *Listen* – from the radio.
They mouthed the words and drew the curtains shyly.
It rained on the examination halls
And on parades and wedding photographs,
On funerals and literary episodes, on rich and idle hours
When we required no occupation but the noise
As rain, like imperial clockwork, ran down in the streets
Or thundered intermittently in vast
Defenestrated Steinways haunted by Debussy.
Rain fell in the hair of all those girls. It fell
In silver columns on the stroke of midnight,
Fell during the rows and the football results
Or while we were sleeping or eating or bathing
Or watching the telephone. Fell in the sea,
In the desert where no rain had fallen for years,
And fell behind the waterfall and on this book
Left out overnight in the garden
To flower illegibly. If there was a dry place
It waited for rain. If there was a damp one
It lay in a state of arousal. And we, my friends,
Were the innumerable heirs to this republic.

– Ours was just a period in the history of rain,
One called by some *The Inundation*
And by others *L'Après-Moi*, since we were young.
The rain is all digression, touching
Everything and nothing, as peremptory
As the Creation, emptying itself
Afresh into this iron river, pooling
In the hand I offer you, and still it seems
Behind the roar and hush there is a chord
We know but never hear, that rain awakes,
And leaves suspended, as between
Acceptance and desire, that calls to us
And, for no reason, speaks on our behalf.

Blizzard

The snow will bring the world indoors, the fall
That saves the Gulf Stream and the Greenland Shelf.
White abolitionist of maps and calendars,
Its Lenten rigour pillowed like a sin, it means
To be the only season, falling always on itself.
To put an end to all analogy, pure cold
That proves what it need never say,
It calls us home again, beneath a drift
In which the figure and the ground collapse –
No more redundancy, no more perhaps.

Look at these attic windowsills, look in the grate –
White after white against the off-white sheets,
The wafers of a pitiless communion
That turns a wood to Mother Russia and the night
To afterlife and then to a snowblind street.
With cataracts and snow-tipped breasts
The mermaids in their brazen lingerie
Wait bravely at the fountain in the square.
Green girls, they think it is their destiny
To offer the ideal to empty air.

Forgive me that I did not understand
That you were actual, not merely art,
That your fidelity was courage, that I failed
To honour you, to recognize your pain,
To grasp that snow once fallen will not fall again.
Now it grows clear: the world is not a place
But an occasion, first of sin and then the wish
That such self-knowledge may be gratified,
While snow continues falling, till we learn
There will be neither punishment nor grace.

Arcadia

I came back to municipal Arcadia
To walk among its foggy linden-groves
And count the line of benches slick with frost
That leads to the black waters of the lake.
There was the landing stage. The garbage scow
Knocked at the shore. The Brylcreemed ferryman
Looked up once from his *Sporting Life* to nod
With the supreme complacency of those
Whose work is waiting patiently forever.
Subtle servitor of Parks and Gardens,
Peerless in the stratagems of absence, Hail!
I wrote the sicknote up for both of us
And then he rowed me out to see the sights.

Was this the destination then, this icy pool
Too shallow for a child, no use at all
To these three pale-skinned nymphs who climbed out now
In navy-blue school costumes and a cloud?
I watched them with a futile tenderness.
The dark, the fair, the fiery, their minds
Had every right to be elsewhere, in fits
That there should be a world, and that it must
Somehow make room for men as well.
They paused a moment, falling silent now,
And looked and did not see, then moved away
Into the dark, still towelling their hair.

The steersman dozed. Snow fell out of the night.
I watched the glasshouse slowly taking shape.
Inside that icy tropic, where the mad,
The unemployed and the irresolute
Could serve their time among the frozen birds,
I saw the young myself still sitting there –
A book of verse, a glass of wine, and thee,
But I could see you'd lost your mind, my dear.
Or who was this bag-lady in the hat?
Why must I pity those I could not help?
I would have saved her if I could, but all
Such declarations show a want of taste,
For poetry deals only in the facts: fact was
That my poor friend was mad and thirty years
Beyond my reach, her terror and her need
Unknown to me, and though she took my arm
For comfort she was sitting with a ghost.

I woke the ferryman. – *Go on. Where next?*
– *There is no next*, he said. *This is the place.*
We slid beneath the footbridge and emerged
Beside an island thick with snowy laurels,
Where he beached. – *Get out and walk from here.*
I entered that enormous miniature
And as in childhood forced my way among
The hypertrophied bushes and the drifts,
Until at what I knew must be the island's heart
I found myself once more beside the lake,
Where he was waiting patiently, as though
We'd never met, and roused himself to push
The iron coffin out from shore again.